REVIVALS: THEIR RISE, PROGRESS AND ACHIEVEMENTS

by Eifion Evans, B.D., Ph.D.

THE history of revivals is the history of God's gracious dealings with men. It is that which Jonathan Edwards styled "the history of redemption", and as such it is the only true history, that is, the only study of the past which is properly "in perspective", for therein is delineated the unfolding and outworking of God's sovereign purpose. To regard it as a mere intellectual exercise therefore betrays a gross underestimate of the meaning, implications, and consequences of revival. The subject is full, not only of interest, but also of instruction, and he who seriously undertakes the study of revivals should not expect to proceed far without becoming intimately involved in and passionately concerned for the issues that arise. There can be no neutrality or sterility here, for this study challenges faith, stimulates prayer, and motivates praise.

It may be necessary in the minds of some to make an apology, or at any rate to give a reason, for proposing the subject at the present time. Evangelical forces are seemingly becoming more concentrated and more prominent, and the need for an effusion of the Holy Spirit in revival, in the opinion of some, is far from desperate or urgent. While more and more attention is being given to men and methods, the significance and importance of the person and work of the Holy Spirit is being gradually diminished. But an enquiry of this kind, perhaps more than any other, demonstrates con-

clusively the deity, holiness, and sovereignty of the third
person of the Trinity. In such a study His gracious manner of
working, in glorifying Christ, in decrying sin and exalting
righteousness, and in conforming men to the divine image, is
forcefully and convincingly brought into focus.

Furthermore, the study of revivals has often been used of
the Holy Spirit to promote an interest in, and a desire for,
another "season of refreshing from the presence of the Lord".
Thus Jonathan Edwards, in urging the publication of a
periodical containing accounts of the progress of the 1740
revival in America, states: "It has been found by experience,
that the tidings of remarkable effects of the power and grace
of God in any place, tend greatly to awaken and engage the
minds of persons in other places."

Now a word as to procedure and purpose. It will be found
that in the main, reference is made to *revivals of the eighteenth
century*. This is an historical enquiry rather than a theological
treatise. Its purpose parallels the several parts of its title,
being an attempt to demonstrate that the Spirit's work is
sovereign in instigating, irresistible in advancing, and sanctifying in establishing, the glory of God in revival.

I DARKNESS BEFORE THE DAWN

Before proceeding to consider the sovereign work of the
Spirit in the rise of revivals, it is necessary to list some
elements in the prevalent situation previously obtaining, and
to indicate their relevance in the light of subsequent events.
At the risk of over-simplification it can be maintained that the
revivals of the sixteenth and eighteenth centuries came to an
apostate, declining, expiring Church, while those of the seventeenth and nineteenth centuries took place against the background of a dormant, listless, and unconcerned Church. The
former situation witnessed the emergence of particular,

leading doctrines and outstanding figures, while the latter
situation was radically altered by invigorated prayer together
with a return to the apostolic preaching of the whole counsel
of God.

A general apostasy

The apostasy of the Church at the beginning of the
eighteenth century is evident from many considerations. In
America the Church allowed an unconverted ministry as valid
and harmless, and allowed an unconverted membership to its
sacramental occasions without examination or enquiry. This
had grave repercussions in that the necessity for regeneration
and a "saving closure with Christ" were seldom insisted upon,
and the vast majority of Church members were strangers to
the covenant of grace. Arminianism was making inroads into
some of the congregations, and its man-centred system was
becoming more and more attractive to the natural mind.
There were however many exceptions, the congregation at
Northampton in 1734 being the most notable, as Edwards
himself wrote: "About this time began the great noise, in this
part of the country, about Arminianism, which seemed to
appear with a very threatening aspect upon the interest of
religion here. The friends of vital piety trembled for fear of
the issue; but it seemed, contrary to their fear, strongly to be
overruled for the promoting of religion. Many who looked on
themselves as in a Christless condition, seemed to be awakened
by it, with fear that God was about to withdraw from the land,
and that we should be given up to heterodoxy and corrupt
principles; and that then their opportunity for obtaining salvation would be past."

Much of the contemporary theological thought in England
and Wales was the product of a philosophical Arminianism,
that is, of Arminian principles developed philosophically so as
to elevate the reason or will of man. The resultant systems of
deism, rationalism and moralism had crippled the Church,

reducing its effectiveness and bringing about a drastic degeneration in its spiritual life. The leaders of the Evangelical Awakening were neither slow nor compromising in their denunciations of these systems.

Such was the theological background for the eighteenth century revival, and it is necessary to further list some of the other elements in the religious situation in the period immediately preceding the great revivals of 1735.

Widespread spiritual darkness

That religion was at a low ebb was the universal complaint of the revivalists as they came to an experience of the gospel and became acquainted with the condition of the Church. While God had not left Himself without witness in any land, it grieved the evangelical leaders to find that those around them who professed religious beliefs, ministers and members alike, were in spiritual darkness and deadness.

The situation at New Londonderry, Pennsylvania, previous to 1740 is depicted by the minister of the parish, and can be regarded as general and typical throughout America.

"The most part seemed to rest contented, and to satisfy their consciences just with a dead formality in religion. A very lamentable ignorance of the main essentials of true practical religion, and the doctrines next related thereto, very generally prevailed. The nature and necessity of the new birth was but little known or thought of. The necessity of a conviction of sin and misery, by the Holy Spirit opening and applying the law to the conscience, in order to a saving closure with Christ, was hardly known at all to most. It was thought that if there was any need of a heart-distressing sight of the soul's danger, and fear of divine wrath, it was only needful for the grosser sort of sinners. There was scarcely any suspicion at all of any danger of depending upon self-righteousness, and not upon the righteousness of Christ alone for salvation."

Jonathan Edwards' analysis of the situation at Northampton in 1734 has more particular reference to the state of the youth. "The greater part seemed to be at that time very insensible of the things of religion, and engaged in other cares and pursuits . . . Licentiousness for some years greatly prevailed among the youth of the town; they were many of them very much addicted to night-walking, and frequenting the tavern, and lewd practices, wherein some, by their example, exceedingly corrupted others. It was their manner very frequently to get together, in conventions of both sexes for mirth and jollity, which they called frolics; and they would often spend the greater part of the night in them, without regard to any order in the families they belonged to."

Meanwhile, in England as early as May 26, 1739, George Whitefield was able to report considerable progress in the revival in the London area, and also that he had found "some thousands of secret ones yet living who have not bowed the knee to Baal." On the other hand, he had not been in Oxford long as a student before he was "solicited to join in their excess of riot with several who lay in the same room"; and that those who desired to live godly in Christ Jesus must suffer persecution—witness the members of the "Holy Club" who received the holy eucharist only after going through "a ridiculing crowd". Whitefield's first sermon was characterized by his plain speaking, and it is significant that two of the practices he denounced were the not-so-innocent entertainments of professing Christians, and the commonly accepted belief in baptismal regeneration.

During the early years of the revival the evangelistic activity of the Welsh revivalists had been confined to the south. Howell Harris visited parts of North Wales in 1740, and he had cause to mourn over the darkness, superstition, and immorality which characterized the land. "This country is all ruined for want of experimental preaching of Christ power-

fully; no gospel light but in a few places . . . went to Tre-
feglwys church to hear—Morris, he preached on 'in keeping of
them there is good reward', the sum of it was do this, be good
and live . . . had a desire to expose him . . . O Lord I can't
help mourning over the darkness of the country of North
Wales! North Wales! Thy guides are blind, the magistrates
are persecutors, and the instruments for Thee are all weak
. . . dreadful things do I hear of all the ministers in these
parts." When he surveyed the situation in North Wales in
February 1741, he could list one dissenting minister in Caer-
narvonshire "full of the love of God", one minister in
Merionethshire, "a very godly man", two such in Mont-
gomeryshire, and the remaining portion of the country is
tragically summed up thus: "I don't find there is any religion
in Anglesey or Flintshire, but near papists; some little dawning
in Denbighshire."

That these accounts were not the exaggerated opinions of
biased men appears from several facts. The leaders of the
revival felt constrained from Scripture premises to raise aloud
their protests against the doctrines and practices of the times.
They saw clearly that multitudes were being deluded by
error and false teaching even within the Church, and they were
grieved at the evils, immorality, and vice which abounded in
the land on all sides. For their uncompromising stand with
regard to these matters and because they sought to lead the
nation, the clergy, and the Church back to New Testament
principles and practices, they were often excluded from the
churches by their enemies, persecuted by the mobs, and
attacked in the pamphlets and printed works of the time.
Nevertheless, God caused them to triumph and many were
added to the Church, having been "born again of God". These
converts soon formed themselves into religious societies for
prayer and fellowship. There could be only one explanation
for these phenomena: God had visited the land in a tremen-

dous outpouring of His Spirit and of power, making that to blossom as the rose which had been formerly a desolated wilderness.

II THE DAWN OF REVIVALS

The 17th and 19th centuries

The seventeenth century was a period of expansion and consolidation for the gospel, when the full implications of the sixteenth century Reformation were being worked out theologically and practically. Much the same was true of the nineteenth century, the churches reaping tremendous benefits from the Evangelical Awakening of the previous century. The condition of the Church varied greatly from time to time and from place to place, but there was no widespread, deep-rooted apostasy in the fullest sense of the word. Rather, the Church experienced times of decline and inactivity interspersed with revival periods of vigorous energy and spiritual prosperity. These revivals were mainly localized, and the human instruments used of the Spirit were generally famous for their work at that place. Here are some obvious examples: David Dickson and the Stewarton revival of 1625; John Livingstone and the Kirk O'Shotts revival in 1630; Richard Baxter's ministry at Kidderminster especially between 1647 and 1660; William C. Burns and Robert Murray M'Cheyne of the Dundee revival in 1839; and David Morgan, whose name is inseparable from Ysbyty Ystwyth and 1859, even though he was used in a far wider sphere than the mountainous region of north Cardiganshire.

The revivals of these two "odd-number" centuries—generally speaking, of course—show distinct characteristics. The Spirit blessed a faithful, zealous ministry in the context of a few godly families, or perhaps a particular sermon at a sacramental occasion. At other times, the godly who had fallen into a deep slumber and become oblivious of their own state and indifferent to that of others, were awakened to pray more frequently and more fervently. It is significant, for example, that in the 1859 revival in Wales, the message which burned in the hearts of Humphrey Jones and David Morgan, the two leading revivalists, was that of Amos 6: 1, "Woe to them that are at ease in Zion". It is also significant that Humphrey Jones, upon his arrival at his home in Cardiganshire in 1858, having given an account of the revival in America from whence he had come, constrained the church to hold prayer meetings every night. Most of the church members had seen or experienced previous revivals—there had been at least fifteen major awakenings in Wales during the previous ten decades—and in setting themselves to pray, their desire was that God would again visit them by His Spirit in a similar fashion. When the churches had been thus led to pray, the preaching of the Word became more powerful, and the substantial truths of the gospel, presented plainly and earnestly, and applied closely and personally, were signally used to the recovery of vast multitudes of men.

The amazing 1830s

One of the most compelling and convincing facts which go to demonstrate the sovereignty of the Holy Spirit in instigating revivals is the simultaneous manner of manifesting His work in various places and in various persons. The eighteen-thirties must surely be reckoned the most amazing decade in modern history for, during those years God graciously visited America, England, Scotland and Wales with powerful revivals. At first these events were apparently unrelated and localized, but within the scope of only a few years they were fused into one mighty awakening, when whole countries and vast tracts of land were submerged in a surge of divine power and momentous spiritual upheaval. It was to Howell Harris a perpetual call to wonder and praise that God had worked thus:

"16 March, 1747 . . . when God visited me and sent me first to speak to people near twelve years ago, I did not know there was a believer living; nor did I as much dream there was a reformation to go on, or that I was to be a preacher; till about two years I heard of a clergyman, one Mr. Rowland, and then a young clergyman here in London that preached four times a day—Mr. Whitefield; and now see how the little cloud has spread over the land, so that God only knows where it will end."

Jonathan Edwards had been converted in the period 1720-22, and had been ordained in 1727, becoming assistant minister to his grandfather over the congregation at Northampton. Evidences of a divine visitation in revival were found in the congregation towards the end of 1733, and during the following year the Holy Spirit's operation was as glorious as it was manifest, so that by the summer of 1735 "the town seemed to be full of the presence of God". In the sovereign purpose of God, similar stirrings were felt in the north of Scotland during the same period. John Balfour was appointed minister of the parish of Nigg, Ross and Cromarty, in 1730. "From that date, Balfour of Nigg became the acknowledged leader of the northern evangelical revivals. In his own parish, from 1730 to 1739, there was a gradual quickening, 'with stops and intermissions', in the spiritual life of the people. In 1739, we notice the unmistakable beginning of a spiritual movement which powerfully affected not only Nigg, but many parishes in Ross and Sutherland, and which is traceable throughout the rest of the century, and well into the next."

The work of the Holy Spirit in conversion was brought to fruition in George Whitefield, Howell Harris, and Daniel Rowland in 1735, in John and Charles Wesley in 1738. Each of these events, as well as being perpetual monuments to the saving grace of God, are also witnesses to the sovereign purpose and plan of God in revival, for from those incidents stems the powerful spate of blessing which revolutionized the spiritual life of the Church in the eighteenth century.

Shortly afterwards, in 1742, William McCullough of Cambuslang and James Robe of Kilsyth were being used of God, having preached consistently and repeatedly on several aspects of the Spirit's work in regeneration in their churches for an appreciable time. By 1747 there were similar revivals on the Continent, and Howell Harris could record in his diary for 14th January of that year the irrepressible progress of the gospel: "Heard refreshing news today of a great revival in France in Montaban by two ministers that preached a month there, and were saved by God from being taken up, and went away. They came through from Geneva. Great was the power of God, and there were gathered 30,000, they came thirty leagues (or ninety miles) to hear."

The revival spread to Ireland in 1745 when "an English soldier in Dublin formed a small society of pious people, and began to preach to them". This society was visited by various Methodist preachers during 1746, and by John Wesley in 1747, so that during Wesley's visit two years later, the preaching of the Word was attended with unusual unction and power, and his voice "could not be heard for the voice of those who cried for mercy, or praised the God of their salvation".

A minister in Holland reported astonishing revival scenes experienced at Nieuwkirk, near Amersfoort, towards the end of 1749, being apparently the climax of a gradual, progressive work of the Spirit. "The Spirit of the Lord began to work in an astonishing manner (during a sermon on Psalm 72: 16 preached on 9th November, 1749); all that had passed before seemed to have been a preparation for greater and more glorious things . . . the trouble of conscience and emotion of affections was general. There was a great lamentation; rivers of tears gushed out, and several fell trembling and astonished to the earth unable to stand by reason of the agony and agitation of their spirits, arising from the sudden, strong impression made upon them of the dreaful state and crying necessity of their souls . . . The following Thursday he (the minister) preached upon Acts 16: 16, 30, 31; where many were brought to a more distinct view of their true state and condition. From that day the work increased beyond description; there is no painting of it to the life; it was a perfect commentary on the second chapter of Acts."

The sovereignty of the Holy Spirit

The Holy Spirit alone could reproduce so exactly in the eighteenth century manifestations such as were seen on the day of Pentecost. What other explanation could be offered for these similar, simultaneous, widespread and powerful blessings, than that the sovereign God was pouring out His Spirit upon all flesh as He purposed and pleased? That which had been found impossible with man was accomplished gloriously, effectively and triumphantly by the Holy Spirit. Human philosophy and morality, pagan superstition, and a corrupt pretence at worship had driven men further from God and had filled the land with darkness, immorality, and hypocrisy. From this hopeless chaos there seemed no deliverance until God intervened in sovereign grace and divine pity, "bringing a clean thing out of an unclean" far beyond human capability, device or intention.

Further illustration of the Spirit's sovereignty in the work of revival is provided by the manner of their beginning. Many factors were involved, sometimes singly and separately, at other times unitedly or as a combination of several such. The Spirit used remarkable providences, sacramental occasions, revival reports, fast days and prayer meetings, as He willed, but supremely it was the preaching of the Word which He especially countenanced and blessed, often together with one or more of the occurrences noted. Jonathan Edwards, the

Tennents, George Whitefield, John Wesley, Daniel Rowland and others like them were called and equipped primarily to preach, and it was in the capacity of preacher that each was most signally blessed and most widely used.

The preaching of a minister in his own parish was often the means honoured by God in a time of revival, as is seen for instance, at New Londonderry in the spring of 1740. The minister, Samuel Blair, wrote his account of the awakening in August 1744: "Religion lay as it were dying, and ready to expire its last breath of life in this part of the visible church. I had some view and sense of the deplorable condition of the land in general; and accordingly the scope of my preaching through that first winter after I came here (1739), was mainly calculated for persons in a natural unregenerate state. I endeavoured, as the Lord enabled me, to open up and prove from His Word, the truths which I judged most necessary for such as were in that state to know and believe in order to their conviction and conversion. I endeavoured to deal searchingly and solemnly with them; and through the concurring blessing of God, I had knowledge of four or five brought under deep convictions that winter . . . The number of the awakened increased very fast. Frequently under sermons there were some newly convicted, and brought into deep distress of soul about their perishing estate. Several would be overcome and fainting; others deeply sobbing, hardly able to contain; and a solemn concern appearing in the countenance of many others. And sometimes the soul-exercises of some (though comparatively but very few) would so far effect their bodies as to occasion some strange unusual bodily motions . . . The general carriage and behaviour of people was soon very visibly altered. Those awakened were much given to reading in the Holy Scriptures and other good books. Excellent books that had lain by much neglected, were then much perused, and lent from one to another; and it was a peculiar satisfaction to people to find how exactly the doctrines they heard daily preached, harmonized with the doctrines contained and taught by great and godly men in other parts and former times."

III THE PROGRESS OF REVIVALS
The preaching of the Word

Revivals thus display great variety in the manner of their beginnings, but preaching seems to be prominent in each case. God's dealing—sometimes drastically—with the parish or local minister often brought about a radical change in the success of the gospel at that place, as the above instances show, and these instances could be multiplied.

The famous Gilbert Tennent was distressed with the want of success in his ministry after being at New Brunswick for about six months. Here are his subsequent experiences:

"It pleased God to afflict me about that time with sickness, by which I had affecting views of eternity. I was then exceedingly grieved that I had done so little for God, and was very desirous to live one half year more, if it was His will, that I might stand upon the stage of the world, as it were, and plead more faithfully for His cause, and take more earnest pains for the conversion of souls. One thing among others pressed me sore; viz. that I had spent much time in conversing about trifles, which might have been spent in examining people's states towards God, and persuading them to turn to Him. After I was raised up to health, I examined many about the grounds of their hope of salvation, which I found in most to be nothing but as the sand. With such I was enabled to deal faithfully and earnestly, warning them of their danger, and urging them to seek converting grace. By this method, many were awakened out of their security; and of those, divers were to all appearances effectually converted, and some that I spoke plainly to were prejudiced. I did then preach much upon original sin, repentance, the nature and necessity of conversion, in a close examinatory and distinguishing way; labouring in the meantime to sound the trumpet of God's judgments, and alarm the secure by the terrors of the Lord, as well as to affect them with other topics of persuasion; which method was sealed by the Holy Spirit in the conviction and conversion of a considerable number of persons."

Many such ministers were stirred up by the Holy Ghost at much the same time, to greater earnestness and faithfulness in their particular duties, and their quickened labours were made effectual to their congregations.

Time and time again in Scotland between 1600 and 1800 God was graciously pleased to pour out a plentiful effusion of the Holy Spirit on sacramental occasions. People would flock to these from a wide area, and the many ministers who attended not only helped at the tables but also preached several times. According to one writer, during this period, "the sacramental assembly and the parochial fellowship meeting were the supreme evangelising agencies; and to one or other of them we can trace all or most of the awakenings and revivals which have quickened the spiritual life of the people."

Fast days or days set apart for prayer sometimes witnessed the first open manifestations of a divine visitation in revival, as was the case at Wrentham, Massachusetts, in February 1741, when the minister preached on Zechariah 12: 10, "And I will pour upon the house of David, and upon the inhabitants of Jerusalem, the spirit of grace and of supplications . . .". "There appeared," according to the account, "especially in the afternoon, a very uncommon attentiveness unto the word, a wonderful tenderness upon the assembly: the tokens of a very serious concern were visible on many faces." The effects spread to neighbouring congregations, the convictions becoming more intense and the conversions more frequent. In August of the same year Halifax, in the county of Plymouth, witnessed a beginning of great things on a similar occasion.

Itinerant preaching

The itinerant ministries of George Whitefield, John Wesley, the Tennents, Howell Harris, and Jonathan Edwards, must also be mentioned as being, under the good blessing of God, instrumental in a large measure to commence awakenings in various parts. Their journals and accounts are full of descriptions of their journeys and the unparalleled success they met with in preaching the gospel. There were not a few who objected to their itinerant labours for various reasons, with the result that they often met opposition from ministers, in that the parish church would be refused to them, and from magistrates who sought to bring them under legal restrictions. The usefulness of their preaching tours, however, can hardly be overestimated, and they contributed in no small measure, under the blessing of God, to the progress as well as to the rise of revivals.

Itinerant preaching accomplished at least two purposes in the progress of the eighteenth century revival. Firstly, it was a means of continued expansion and propagation by preaching; and secondly, it was the means of consolidation and instruction of the converts in the religious societies by exhortation.

The leaders of the revival began itinerating for a variety of reasons. While on a visit to Bristol, George Whitefield was called upon during a service to address the congregation, and he instantly complied with the request. More invitations followed, and each he regarded as a divine call to preach the gospel. Furthermore, the remarkable success which followed this ministry, first in Bristol, and later in London, could only be interpreted in Whitefield's mind as being a clear indication of its validity, expediency and usefulness in the divine purpose. This work commenced early in 1737 in Bristol, and by September, in London, Whitefield could record that "for near three months successively, there was no end of the people flocking to hear the Word of God".

To Howell Harris likewise the urge to itinerate came from within, an irresistible consequence of the nature of his spiritual experience of God's free and sovereign grace. Soon after his conversion on Whit-Sunday 1735 he set up family worship in his own home, and visited the neighbouring farms and houses. Upon his return home after an abortive attempt to settle at Oxford for study, he busied himself with "going about" amongst the nearby parishes spreading the message which "did so burn" in his soul, giving him no rest "day or night, without doing something" for his God and Saviour. His own account is particularly striking. "After my return, I was occupied in going from house to house until I had visited nearly the whole of the parish in which I was born, together with some of the neighbouring ones. The people began now to assemble in vast numbers, so that the houses in which I addressed them were too small for the congregations. The Word was attended with such power, that many cried out on the spot for the pardon of their sins." That account refers to 1736; by 1742 his zeal and fervour had by no means diminished, as this extract from his diary for 4th September of that year will show : "I was often led to cry : We are about soul's work! Eternity work and God's work. There is no jesting with God."

Daniel Rowland's usefulness was by no means confined to his ministry at Llangeitho. It is true of him, as it was to be of Thomas Charles of Bala later, that his chief contribution to the rise and progress of the revival was his amazing labours at that preaching centre. From Llangeitho and Bala there radiated forth to the rest of the Principality such an influence for good that hitherto has never been surpassed. Daniel Rowland, however, had commenced preaching outside his own parish by August 1737 as Howell Harris heard him at Devynock, Breconshire, on the 13th of that month. By August the following year he had been to at least two parishes in Carmarthen-shire, and by 1740 Daniel Rowland had visited North Wales at least once.

John Wesley, being refused access to many pulpits in London, began his itineraries in 1738, and fifty years later he could write in retrospect, "God has been pleased to bless the itinerant plan . . . it must not be altered . . . I hope it will remain till our Lord comes to reign upon earth."

The visit of Jonathan Edwards to Enfield was the beginning of a revival which spread over a wide area. On that occasion, 8th July, 1741, he preached on "sinners in the hands of an angry God", basing his remarks on Deuteronomy 32: 35, ". . . their foot shall slide in due time . . ." "Before the sermon was ended, the assembly appeared deeply impressed and bowed down with an awful conviction of their sin and danger. There was such a breathing of distress and weeping, that the preacher was obliged to speak to the people and desire silence, that he might be heard. This was the beginning of the same great and prevailing concern in that place, with which the colony in general was visited."

No effort against such itinerant ministries was successful, and God prospered the work under the hands of the ministers so mightily that it grew beyond all imaginable proportions. When God wills success no man can impose failure.

Field preaching

Field preaching was in effect only the inevitable consequence of itinerant preaching. Whereas it was found by the leaders of the revival to be a necessity because of closed churches, they came to regard it as nothing short of the providential ordering of God. In fact, the revival which their enemies desired to quench and end, prospered and progressed all the more because of it. Furthermore, it would have been impossible to accommodate the tens of thousands which flocked to hear the Word of God had not Whitefield and the others taken to preaching in the open air.

The "ice" was broken on 17th February, 1739, when Whitefield preached to some 200 colliers at Kingswood, and his joyful comments were these: "I believe I never was more acceptable to my Master than when I was standing to teach those hearers in the open fields. Some may censure me; but if I thus pleased men, I should not be the servant of Christ." A few months later he noted in his *Journal* what must have been, to him, ample justification for that memorable decision to preach in the open air: "Thousands at the great day will have reason to bless God for field-preaching." By May of 1748 the desirability and usefulness of field preaching had so impressed itself upon Howell Harris's mind that he was concerned lest anything should arise to deny the revivalists this means of publishing the gospel tidings. "If we'll be obliged to license ourselves and houses, it will cramp the work and stop field-preaching."

Religious societies

Another important factor in the progress of the revival was the setting up of the religious societies, or, as Whitefield described them in 1742 to the Bishop of Bangor, "little fellowship meetings, where some well-meaning people meet together, simply to tell what God has done for their souls." The first society was formed in Breconshire by Howell Harris as early as 1736, and by 1739 about thirty of them had been organized and regulated in South Wales, "in imitation of the Societies which Dr. (Josiah) Woodward had given an account of."

These religious societies were set up by the revivalists in an attempt to ensure the spiritual growth and well-being of their converts. Their meetings were times of prayer, fellowship, and Bible study, and very often would include the singing of a hymn or psalm, followed by the leader's exposition of a passage of Scripture, or catechism, together with an opportunity for discussion, and the sharing of spiritual experiences and difficulties. Inasmuch therefore that by these means the young converts were nurtured in spiritual things, being the means of their growth in grace and in knowledge of Jesus Christ, their contribution to the progress and eventual achievement of the revival was an important one. Very often they supplied a deficiency which the parish clergy were either unable or unwilling to supply.

Religious literature

The religious literature produced by the Evangelical Awakening added further fuel to the fires of the revival. Between 1740 and 1745 accounts of the success of the gospel in various parts appeared in a weekly periodical bearing the title successively of *The Christian's Amusement, The Weekly History, An Account of the Progress of the Gospel,* and *The Christian History.* The Scottish counterparts of those London publications were *The Glasgow Weekly History,* and James Robe's *Monthly History.* A similar periodical appeared in Boston in America, under the title *The Christian History.*

Extracts from these were read in the societies on "letter days" and in many instances quickened interest in the revival's progress, and stimulated prayer for the revival's continued success. They consisted chiefly of letters sent by the leading revivalists or portions of their journals. The publication of the latter, by Whitefield and John Wesley in particular, together with the publication of their sermons, had the same effects, as did also the appearance in print of the hymns of Charles Wesley and William Williams. One Welsh revival, that of 1763, received tremendous impetus from the appearance in print of a collection of William Williams' hymns, and gave rise to outbursts of praise and rejoicing which were hardly equalled anywhere during the whole of the eighteenth century. The Welsh catechisms of Griffith Jones, Llanddowror, proved eminently profitable to the religious societies and in the "charity schools". The latter could be regarded as the religious nurseries of the revival in Wales, and their work was carried on by Thomas Charles of Bala in the Sunday schools.

Doctrinal emphasis

Such were some of the leading factors in the progress of the eighteenth century revival and it remains only to outline some of the emergent characteristics as the work progressed. The leading figures rose to prominence at an early stage, and it was not long before their doctrinal emphasis also became apparent. Thomas Prince of Boston defined the broad principles of the revival in his statement concerning the work in his own parish: "Nor, in all the preaching of the instruments of this work in town, did I ever hear any teach to follow impulses or any religious impressions but of the Word of God upon our minds, affections, wills, and consciences; and which, agreeable to the Holy Scriptures, the most famous reformers and Puritan ministers, both in England, Scotland, and New-England, have in their writings taught us. As to the doctrinal principles of those who continue in our congregations, and have been the subjects of the late revival, they are the same as they have been instructed in all along, from the Westminster Assembly's *Shorter Catechism*."

A similar statement is given by the minister of Golspie (Sutherland) which was blessed with an outpouring of the Holy Spirit in November 1743: "The terrors of the Lord denounced in his Word against the wilful transgressors of his holy laws, and the impenitent unbelieving despisers of his gospel grace; the impossibility of salvation on the score of self-righteousness; the absolute necessity of the efficacious influences of the grace and Spirit of God, in order to a vital union with Christ by faith, for righteousness and salvation; that all the blessings of the new covenant, freely given by the Father to the elect, and purchased for them by the sufferings and death of Christ the Son, are effectually applied to them by the Holy Ghost—these were the doctrines insisted on to the people of this congregation."

Stress on regeneration

If, however, one doctrine received more prominence than any other during the eighteenth century awakening, it was that of regeneration. It was as characteristic of that movement of the Spirit, as justification by faith was of the Reformation of the sixteenth century. It seems to have been the doctrine, above any other, which was honoured of the Holy Spirit during the whole period of eighteenth century revivals. From 1734, when "a ray of divine light . . . darted in" upon the soul of George Whitefield, when he knew that he had to be "a new creature", until the Moulin revival of 1798 this particular doctrine was kept to the fore. Thus Whitefield refers to the subject at least forty-six times in his *Journals* in the decade 1734-44, while, during the same period, justification by faith is mentioned about eight times. It is not without significance that his first publication as early as August 1737 was a sermon on "The Nature and Necessity of our New Birth in Jesus Christ, in order to Salvation". The fact that it passed through at least three editions before the end of the same year, having "sold well to persons of all denominations and dispersed very much at home and abroad", lends added weight to the contention.

The fact that preaching on regeneration was so universally blessed of the Holy Spirit secures for it further recognition as a salient doctrine in the revival. The minister of Hopewell and Amwell in New Jersey preached for six months on the subjects of conviction and conversion before the Holy Spirit's powerful influence descended upon his congregations in May 1739. The same truths were insisted upon to the congregation at New Londonderry before their "seasons of refreshing" in 1740. Multitudes were affected under the preaching of White-field on the subject at Boston in 1740. William McCulloch had been over ten years at Cambuslang before he decided to preach on those subjects "which tend most directly to explain the nature, and prove the necessity of regeneration". This he did for about a year before February, 1742, when the truths he had been preaching and insisting upon became a reality in the experiences of vast numbers of his congregation. The same was true at Kilsyth under James Robe's ministry in 1740, and at Llangeitho, under Daniel Rowland's ministry, in 1781.

These facts must surely indicate that even as the Holy Spirit in His sovereign choice used certain human instruments, so also He signally honoured certain doctrines, not exclusively, but more especially. The choice is necessarily His and bears no robot-like imitation. The impulse must come from Him, even as the power accompanying the Word must be ascribed to Him.

Physical manifestations

The severity and intensity of the convictions during revivals deserve a comment. These were not constant but fluctuated from place to place. There were amazing conversions in people of all ages. The revival manifestations or phenomena such as physical prostrations, crying out, fainting, and so on, were witnessed in many places both in Europe and America. They were objected to by some and counterfeited by others. Jonathan Edwards' *Treatise on the Religious Affections* was an attempt to answer the objections and to correct the abuses attendant upon such phenomena. Perhaps the most amazing account of such incidents is given by Jonathan Edwards himself in alluding to the revival experiences at Northampton in 1741: "The months of August and September were the most remarkable of any this year, for appearances of conviction and conversion of sinners, and great revivings, quickenings, and comforts of professors, and for extraordinary external effects of these things. It was a very frequent thing to see a house full of outcries, faintings, convulsions, and such like, both with distress, and also with admiration and joy. It was not the manner here to hold meetings all night, as in some places, nor was it common to continue them till very late in the night: but it was pretty often, so that there were some that were so affected, and their bodies so overcome, that they could not go home, but were obliged to stay all night at the house where they were."

Whitefield obviously experienced some difficulty at first in accepting these phenomena as being truly the work of God and not of the devil, for John Wesley had occasion to reprimand him of thus censuring the sovereignty and power of the Holy Spirit. Wesley notes in his *Journal* for 7th July, 1739: "I had an opportunity to talk with him of those outward signs which had so often accompanied the inward work of God. I found his objections were chiefly grounded on gross misrepresentations of matter of fact. But the next day he had an opportunity of informing himself better: for no sooner had he begun (in the application of his sermon) to invite all sinners to believe in Christ, than four persons sunk down close to him, almost in the same moment. One of them lay without either sense or motion; a second trembled exceedingly; the third had strong convulsions all over his body, but made no noise, unless by groans; the fourth, equally convulsed, called upon God, with strong cries and tears. From this time, I trust, we shall all suffer God to carry on His own work in the way that pleaseth Him."

Such evidences of the work of the Spirit which resulted in conversion and sanctification, then, demonstrate the intensity of the revival, and the irresistible power of the Spirit in bringing the truth to the mind with such reality and force. The vast majority of occurrences of this nature could only be attributed to the divine authorship.

That is not to say that there were no spurious conversions or false manifestations; but they appear to have been soon detected and exposed, as is seen from the following report relating to New Londonderry: "They endeavoured just to get themselves affected by sermons, and if they could come to weeping, or get their passions so raised as to incline them to vent themselves by cries, now they hoped they were got under convictions, and were in a very hopeful way; and afterwards, they would speak of their being in trouble, and aim at complaining of themselves, but seemed as if they knew not well how to do it, nor what to say against themselves. And thus, much in such a way as this, some appeared to be pleasing themselves just with an imaginary conversion of their own making."

Unworthy and detrimental incidents of this nature were, however, comparatively few, and lost significance in the great weight of testimony concerning the more valid and genuine experiences of innumerable others. John Wesley's comment in 1745 well deserves to be quoted here: "Do you delay fixing your judgment till you see a work of God without any stumbling block attending it? That never was yet, nor ever will . . . And scarce ever was there such a work of God before, with so few as have attended this."

Some of the factors involved in the progress of revivals have been outlined, and together they serve to emphasise the omnipotence of God in His gracious dealings with men. Revivals, therefore, in their rise and progress are supremely the work of the Holy Spirit. Their effects and achievements are glorious;

being the Lord's doing, they are marvellous in the eyes of all who see them.

IV THE FRUITS OF REVIVALS

What, then, were the achievements?   The revivals of the eighteenth century brought about the overthrow of the prevailing philosophical systems which pretended to a theological character. That philosophy which is the product of the natural mind and of worldly wisdom is quite incompatible with "the simplicity which is in Christ", and it was from this latter position that the evangelical leaders of the eighteenth century sought to lead the Church. They offered no apology for doing so, they merely yielded to an inward compulsion to preach the gospel of Christ in simple Scriptural terms. They therefore held forth the free offer of salvation by grace, preaching plainly, closely and personally the substantial truths of the New Testament with zeal, earnestness and fervour, being constrained by the love of Christ to do so. "Two things exceeding needful in ministers," says Jonathan Edwards, "as they would do any great matters to advance the kingdom of Christ, are *zeal* and *resolution*." He continues: "Zeal and courage will do much in persons of but an ordinary capacity; but especially would they do great things, if joined with great abilities. If some great men who have appeared in our nation, had been as eminent in divinity as they were in philosophy, and had engaged in the Christian cause with as much zeal and fervour as some others have done, and with a proportional blessing of heaven, they would have conquered all Christendom, and turned the world upside down."

Deism, Socinianism, and Unitarianism were swept aside as the revival spread, and many of those churches which had been under their shadow were restored into full gospel light and liberty. A faithful ministry returned to the land which ensured the safety and prosperity of the churches for many years.

Spiritual experiences

Not the least of the blessings which ensued from the revival were the elevated spiritual experiences of the members of Christ's Church, and the sense of the divine love which pervaded the churches. By 1736 Jonathan Edwards was able to list some of the achievements of the 1734 revival at Northampton in this way: "Persons after their conversion often speak of religious things as seeming new to them; that preaching is a new thing; that it seems to them they never heard preaching before; that the Bible is a new book: they find there new chapters, new psalms, new histories, because they see them in a new light . . . Some who before were very rough in their temper and manners, seemed to be remarkably softened and sweetened. And some have had their souls exceedingly filled, and overwhelmed with light, love, and comfort, long since the work of God has ceased to be so remarkably carried on in a general way . . . There is still a great deal of religious conversation continued in the town, amongst young and old; a religious disposition appears to be still maintained amongst our people, by their holding frequent private religious meetings . . . we still remain a reformed people, and God has evidently made us a new people."

Sanctifying effects

This visible reformation in morality and society of which Jonathan Edwards speaks was not confined to his congregation, but appeared universally wherever the Holy Spirit had been poured out in revival. They can best be defined as sanctifying effects, the Holy Spirit working to the glory of God in churches and communities through the changed lives of their members. In answer to several queries from the Presbytery of Aberdeen regarding the revival of 1839 at Dundee, Robert Murray McCheyne could write in 1841: "The Sabbath is now observed with greater reverence than it used to be! and there seems to be far more of a solemn awe upon the minds of men than formerly. The private meetings for prayer have spread a sweet influence over the place. There is far more solemnity in the house of God; and it is a different thing to the people now from what it once was. Any minister of spiritual feeling can discern that there are many praying people in the congregation. When I first came here, I found it impossible to establish Sabbath schools while, very lately, there were instituted with ease nineteen such schools, that are well taught and well attended."

These effects and achievements were typical of those attained irrespective of country or time or instrument. The Holy Spirit was at work, glorifying Christ in the salvation of sinners, bringing men into subjection, by His powerful operations, to the truth as it is in Jesus, and establishing that righteousness in a nation which alone exalts it.

Whole communities transformed

In the experience of the Church the eighteenth century was one continuous flow of revivals, which the Holy Spirit moulded from its infinite variety of situations, circumstances, impossibilities, instruments, and conditions, into one great healing stream. The leading revivalists were "men of like passions as we are", subject to errors, sins, and temptations, but the Holy Spirit used them in spite of their limitations and failings. As they preached, the Holy Spirit accompanied the Word with power and it became the "savour of life" to many. The deadness and barrenness which had prevailed in the Church, and the indifference and immorality which had abounded in the world, could not withstand the surge of spiritual life which flowed through mere men, but issued from a divine source. Whole communities were affected and transformed, great churches were reformed and invigorated, vast countries took on a new aspect. From this movement of God's Spirit new missionary enterprises were born, philanthropic institutions blossomed forth, and ecclesiastical foundations were consolidated. The repercussions of the movement not only traversed continents but also periods and ages, giving cause for generations to come to praise God, and securing for them a priceless heritage.

Our greatest need!

Alas! that it is necessary to bemoan in these days the scarcity of such divine visitations as were so frequent in the eighteenth century! Is it not to the grief of Christians today that so few know "the years of the right hand of the most High", that so few have witnessed and experienced those blessed effusions of the Holy Spirit which so radically altered the condition of God's Church and the appearance of human society? Thomas Charles of Bala saw many such wondrous works of God during his lifetime, and he expressed it as his full persuasion, "that unless we are favoured with frequent revivals, and a strong, powerful work of the Spirit of God, we shall in a great degree, degenerate, and have only a *'name to live'*: religion will soon lose its vigour; the ministry will hardly retain its lustre and glory; and iniquity will, in consequence, abound."

How alarming! How miserable! How poverty-stricken must be the condition of Christ's Church today, when so many years have passed without a revival! Oh! may the Holy Spirit grant to His people in these days that they shall see and realize their state, and be led by the Spirit of adoption to cry to their heavenly Father: *O God, how long shall the adversary reproach? Shall the enemy blaspheme thy name for ever? Why withdrawest thou thy hand, even thy right hand? Pluck it out of thy bosom. (Psa. 74: 10, 11.) Awake, awake, put on strength, O arm of the Lord; awake, as in the ancient days, in the generations of old. (Isa. 51: 9.)*